"Looking Back... Unexplained"
(Collection of Ghostly Tales and Haunts)

Jo Ann Atcheson Gray

Contents

" *Looking Back...*
Unexplained "

(Collection of Ghostly Tales and Haunts)

Chapter 1

A Ghost in the Closet

The old house creaked like a ship lost at sea, its floorboards whispering secrets to anyone brave enough to listen. Green ivy clung to the weathered brick, and the windows, clouded with years of dust, seemed to hide a world of memories. Ella stood in the middle of her new, guest bedroom, her heart pounding as she took in the soothing shadows that seemed to dance in the fading light. Moving to Willow Creek had felt like a fresh, new start, but the echoes of her past clung to her like a damp fog. Memories of her husband, who had passed away from a heart condition just a few years back, after his loss, Ella relocated to New Orleans from North Carolina. She'd spent the last week here unpacking boxes, stacking books and arranging her few personal belongings with the hope of making the space feel like home, but something about this one room unsettled her.

As the sun dipped lower, casting elongated shadows across the walls, Ella turned her attention to the vacant closet. It loomed ominously in the corner of the room, its darkened door slightly ajar, as if inviting her to explore the secrets within. She had noticed it the first time she stepped inside; it seemed out of place in an otherwise bright room, the heavy wood and intricate carvings too ornate for a simple guest bedroom.

Taking a deep breath, Ella approached the mysterious closet. The air felt slightly cooler near the heavy door, and a slight shiver ran down her spine. It was ridiculous, she assured herself. Ghosts were not real, but as she reached for the handle, her hand still trembled with a slight fear. With a swift tug, the door swung open. Inside, it was surprisingly spacious, lined with old wooden shelves that held only a few old, dusty trinkets... a dusty, faded hand mirror, a moth-eaten hat, and a faded, black and white photograph. She grabbed the old mirror as she blew the dust from the withered, broken glass, the mere reflection of her auburn hair and green eyes looking back at her, placing it back in its place she picked up the old photo, wiping away the mere dust it held to reveal a family smiling back at her, their faces blurred by an ancient time.

Suddenly, a soft sound echoed from the back of the closet, a rustling, like fabric brushing against fabric. Ella's heart raced as she turned her head sharply toward the faint sound. "Hello?" she whispered, her voice barely steady. The house seemed to hold its breath, and for a moment, all she could hear was the faint, fast thudding of her own heart. The rustling stopped, leaving an unsettling silence in its wake. Ella stepped back, confused, her instincts screaming at her to just leave the mere closet alone, but her curiosity held her in place. She felt strangely drawn to this closet now, as if something inside of it was calling to her. She took a tentative step closer, further into the closet, peering into the mere shadows, "Is anyone there?" she asked nervously, half-hoping for a response, half-dreading it. Just as she was about to turn away, giving up, she saw a faint flicker of movement in the corner of her eye. A shape shifted, just out of reach. Her breath caught in her throat, "Show yourself!"

The closet seemed to tremble, and with a sudden rush, the air seemed to grow heavier, colder. From the dark shadows of the closet, emerged a figure, pale and translucent, its features barely discernible. Ella gasped, stumbling back as the ghostly apparition flickered in and out of focus. "Help me," it whispered faintly, over and over, a voice like the wind rustling through the leaves.

In that moment, Ella knew she had stumbled upon something beyond her mere understanding, something that would tether her to the past, to the very heart of the old house itself, and as the faint figure faded back into the shadows of the closet, Ella realized that her fresh, new start might just be intertwined with a haunting mystery that was waiting to unfold. 'Either ghosts were actually real, or she was going insane' was her mere thoughts.

Chapter 2

A Haunting in New Orleans

Ella stood in the vibrant heart of New Orleans, her senses overwhelmed by the sights, sounds, and scents of the city. The air was thick with the mere aroma of beignets and shrimp gumbo, and jazz melodies danced through the crowded streets, drawing her into a rhythm that felt both foreign and familiar. It had been a week since she first encountered the ghost in her closet, and though she had returned to Willow Creek, her mere thoughts still lingered on the mysteries of the past. Determined to seek answers, she found herself wandering into the French Quarter, where the historic buildings wore their age with great pride, each facade a story etched in the brick and wrought iron. The sun hung low in the sky, casting a warm golden glow over the streets, and Ella felt a magnetic pull toward a quaint little shop nestled between two larger buildings, 'Madame Celeste's Curiosities'.

The fragile, black bell above the squeaking door jingled as she stepped inside. The air was heavy with the mere scent of burning incense, and shelves overflowed with strange trinkets, crystals, and dusty tomes. At the back, a woman with silver-streaked hair and piercing green eyes sat behind a cluttered, worn counter, her gaze fixed on Ella as if she had been expecting her.

"Welcome, my dear," Madame Celeste said, her voice smooth as molasses. "I sense you have come seeking something more than mere curiosities."

Ella hesitated but felt an undeniable urge to confide in this strange lady, "I think... I think I saw a ghost, an actual real ghost. In my house, my new house, and I feel like it is connected to something deeper, something from the past."

Madame Celeste nodded knowingly, "New Orleans is a city steeped in much history, though some may be dark, where the past always lingers like the humidity in the mere air. Spirits, some good, some evil, often wander these very streets, drawn by much unfinished business, cruel fates, and lost memories."

"Is that why you have so many, strange... items in this shop?" Ella asked, as she gestured her hand toward the room of the little shop. "To somehow connect with them?"

"Indeed, my dear. Each object holds its own story, a fragment of someone's existence, but it's not just the objects... it's the mere energy that they carry." Madame Celeste explained, leaning forward, her green eyes sparkling with intrigue. "Tell me more about your ghostly experience."

Ella recounted the encounter in her guest bedroom closet, the rustling, the faint figure, the plea for help that it whispered. As she spoke, Madame Celeste's expression grew serious, her brows furrowing slightly. "That energy you felt, my dear," she said, "it is a connection to the past, a dark past, perhaps, a lingering echo of someone who once lived in that old house. The spirit may be lost, searching for some sort of closure. You must try to understand, not all spirits mean us any harm; some simply need our help or just wish to share their stories."

"What do I do?" Ella asked, her heart starting to race at the mere thought of returning to her new home and speaking to a spirit. "How can I help it?"

"First, you must be completely open to the mere experience," Madame Celeste advised. "You'll need to create a space for communication, a place where the spirit feels safe, trusting, to reveal its truth to you. Gather items that might resonate with you and that belong to your home, along with anything that might connect to the spirit. Then, sit quietly, and simply invite the spirit to share its story with you."

Ella nodded slowly, feeling a mix of fear and determination. "I will try. Thank you."

As she turned to leave the little shop, Madame Celeste called after her, "And remember, my dear, not all that is lost seeks to be found. Approach with care, caution, and trust your inner instincts."

The streets outside were alive with much activity, but Ella felt a newfound sense of purpose. The ghost in her closet was not just an anomaly; it was a bridge to something deeper, a connection that seemed to transcend time. She made her way back to Willow Creek, with the silver-haired lady's words still lingering in her thoughts and the ghostly figure still fresh in her mind. Once home, she rummaged through all her belongings, collecting items that felt significant, a fragile, vintage locket that her grandmother had given her, a small journal filled with her thoughts, and a pillar candle, its wax a deep, calming ivory, along with the old, black and white photograph from the guest bedroom closet and the broken hand mirror. She arranged them all on the floor of the guest bedroom near the closet, creating a circle that felt somewhat sacred. As dusk settled, Ella lit the pillar candle, its flame flickering in the dim, faint light. She closed her eyes, taking a deep breath, and opened her heart. "If you are here," she whispered nervously, "please, I invite you to share your story."

The air grew still, calm, and the shadows seemed to lengthen in the room, wrapping around her like a cloak. She felt a presence, warm and sensitive, as if someone was watching her. The very walls of the old house seemed to be listening, and then, a soft rustling echoed from the closet, a sound just like before. Ella opened her eyes with slight fear bubbling in her stomach. "Help me," the voice whispered again, more urgent this time, threading through the mere stillness like a heartbeat.

Ella's pulse quickened, but she remained steady, "I am here. I want to help you. Please, tell me what you need. How can I help you?"

As the pillar candle flickered, the faint figure began to take shape in the doorway of the closet, and Ella steeled herself for the revelation that was about to unfold, a mere haunting that intertwined her life with a past life that was long forgotten, leading her deeper into the mysteries of Willow Creek and beyond.

Chapter 3

A Collection of Ghostly Tales and Haunts

The candlelight flickered, casting elongated shadows on the walls of the guest bedroom where Ella was kneeling in the middle of the circle of trinkets, the mere air felt cool, charged with much energy now, as if the very fabric of her reality was stretching thin between herself and the faint spirit in the doorway of the closet. Ella focused, her pounding in her chest, ready to listen.

As the faint figure stepped forward, Ella was frightful, ready to run, but she forced herself to remain calm, steady. The was filled with a shimmering light now, that slowly coalesced into the form of a young woman. The spirit's ethereal features were framed by long, flowing hair of blonde waves, and her dress, though tattered, held an air of elegance that hinted at another time in history. Ella could see the mere sadness in her fragile ghostly eyes.

"I am Adeline," the spirit whispered, her voice fragile, soft, a mere echo that felt both distant and intimate. "I need your help to remember."

"Remember what?" Ella asked, curiosity piqued. "What happened to you?"

Adeline hesitated, as she hovered in front of Ella, her gaze drifting toward the window as if searching for something lost in the distance. "I lived in this very house long ago... before it was abandoned, forgotten. My family... we were woven into the very fabric of this place, but such tragedy stole my story, leaving only dark shadows behind."

Ella felt a cool shiver run down her spine, "What kind of tragedy?"

"A fire," Adeline murmured, her voice barely above a whisper. "One fateful night, it consumed us all, and I was trapped within this closet, this house, within these very walls, unable to ever leave. My family... they never found peace. I was left to wander, searching for a way to remember who I was and what all I lost."

"Your family..." Ella began, her heart still racing, yet now, aching for the spirit, "Do you want to help me, guide me, in finding your family?"

Adeline nodded, her expression a mixture of hope and despair. "Yes. They are scattered, their stories buried beneath time. I cannot rest until I can piece together exactly what happened to us."

Ella felt a sense of purpose blossom within her. This was really happening. "I will help you, Adeline, I promise, but how?"

"Take the photograph. Seek the truth, the tales," Adeline replied, her faint voice growing stronger, determined. "There are many stories within this very town, others just like me, tied to the places they loved. If you only listen, they will guide you."

As the pillar candle flickered, illuminating the young woman's face, Ella could see the spirit's determination, her mere sadness, in her eyes. " I will try," she vowed, with confidence, "I will try to find them, and your family."

With that mere promise, Adeline's form began to shimmer, her features blurring as she prepared to withdraw back into the closet.

"But be careful, cautious," the spirit warned, her faint voice echoing with urgency, "Not all spirits are as gentle as I am. Some are bound by much anger and despair."

"I will be very cautious," Ella whispered under her breath, as her heart still raced in her chest, "You can trust in me, Adeline."

With a final bright flicker of light, Adeline faded back into the closet, leaving Ella alone in the dimly lit array of the pillar candle within the room, her mind swirling with the mere possibilities. She needed to learn more about the house, the mere history of Willow Creek, and the stories told, that lay hidden just beneath the surface. Ella reached for the old photograph of Adeline's family and blew out the pillar candle.

The next day, Ella set off on her quest. She began at the local library, a grand building with tall, arched windows that filtered sunlight onto many rows of dusty shelves. The air inside was comfortably cool and slightly musty, filled with the scent of old paper and ink. She approached the librarian, a kind woman with silver hair pulled back into a neat, tight bun.

"I'm looking for any information on the history of my old house that I just recently moved into," Ella said, her slight excitement containing itself within her, "It's Willow Creek Manor. Do you have any old archives or records?"

"Ah, Willow Creek Manor," the silver-haired librarian replied, her sharp eyes sparkling with slight intrigue, "It has quite the history. Follow me."

Ella followed the woman to a back room filled with old, faded records, maps, and fragile, antique books. The librarian pulled out a large, leather-bound volume. "This is the very journal of the original owner of the house, his name was Thomas. He built the manor over a century ago. There are many strange tales woven into its very walls."

As Ella flipped through the vintage, fragile pages, she uncovered snippets of mere life that was in the old house so long ago, festive gatherings, the mere laughter of children running through its halls, and the quiet moments that seemed to follow, but as she turned the delicate pages, she found a chilling entry dated to one stormy night, detailing a massive fire that took place there, taking Adeline's family. The last entry was frantic, filled with much fear and urgency, ending abruptly with a smear of ink.

"Well, that explains why this old, leather-bound volume was black, worn and smelled of smoke. What exactly happened on that night?" Ella wondered aloud, a faint whisper to herself, feeling the weight of a past history pressing down on her now.

The librarian sensing Ella's curiosity, added. "Many locals of the area believe that the house is very haunted by the spirits of those who perished in that fire. Their stories still linger, waiting to be told. The old manor was rebuilt over time as many different owners passed through it, but none actually stayed there very look, due to all the hauntings."

Ella's heart skipped a beat, it seemed, "I need to find out more. Are there any more records of any of the other families, individuals, connected to the manor? Rest assured, I am not leaving my house, no matter how many ghosts might dwell inside of it."

"Certainly, there are," the silver-haired librarian replied, her eyes wide with a slight shock at Ella's words, as she pulled out another stack of old documents. "Many families lived there after the hose burned, leaving their own marks, some joyful, some tragic."

As Ella pored over the old documents, she learned of the different families that had came and went, each with their own past stories of love, loss, and much heartache. There was the Hattie family, who celebrated many holidays in the grand dining room, only to be shattered by the loss of a child, and the Dupe family, who turned the attic into a child's playroom, only to be haunted by faint whispers in the night. Each old tale resonated with Ella, weaving a tapestry of much sorrow and hope that mirrored Adeline's story. She felt a slight connection to all these spirits, as if they were guiding her through their collective grief, just as Adeline had told her, urging her to remember what they had forgotten.

Determined, Ella left the library with a newfound knowledge, a new sense of reasoning. She would gather these old stories, piece them together, and in doing so, help Adeline find her deceased family, and perhaps, give all the other spirits that may dwell in the old manor, a voice as well, along with setting them free, to find their peace in their afterlife.

As she hurried home, the sun dipped below the horizon, and shadows lengthened across the cobblestone streets. Ella knew that this small journey would be fraught with challenges, but she felt a fire ignite within her, one that matched the spirit of Adeline and longing for remembrance. Ella hadn't dwelt on the loss of her husband since she started this quest. As she reached Willow Creek Manor, she could almost hear all the whispers of the past calling out to her, urging her to uncover the secrets of the house and the lives that had once filled its very halls. The mere collection of ghostly tales and many haunts was only just beginning, and Ella was ready to embrace the hauntings that awaited her.

Chapter 4

The Spirit World

The mere air at Willow Creek felt different the night after Ella's visit to the local library, thick with anticipation as she prepared to delve deeper into the spirit world of the old manor. She lit the pillar candle once more, its mere flame casting a warm glow that flickered against the old walls, creating a sanctuary for the past stories she hoped to uncover.

Ella settled into her makeshift circle of personal items, feeling the weight of her locket, journal, and the pillar candle, along with the old photograph of Adeline and her family, as they all connected her to both the living and the dead. Taking a deep breath, she closed her eyes, same as before, focusing on her intention. "Adeline," she whispered, "if you are here, please guide me."

At first, there was only silence, but then, a gentle cool breeze seemed to pass through the guest bedroom, the pillar candle's flame dancing wildly as if responding to a presence, as Ella opened her eyes. She felt a rush of energy, a familiar warmth enveloping her. Turning her gaze, there stood Adeline, more vividly than before, her mere translucent form shimmering like sunlight on water.

"You've begun your journey," Adeline said, her faint voice a soft melody that wrapped around Ella like a comforting embrace. "I can sense the mere stories within you now, waiting to emerge."

"What do I need to do, to know?" Ella asked, her heart aching to find the answers. "How can I help you and your family now?"

"To understand the mere spirit world, you must first understand your own inner heart," Adeline replied, stepping closer. "Every spirit here has a story, a reason for remaining tethered to this realm, this house. Our lives are intertwined with our past, living emotions, and those mere emotions can bind us to this place, these moments, and each other."

Ella nodded, trying to understand Adeline's words, feeling the truth of them resonate within her, "What about all the other spirits who may dwell here? The other ones who are tied to this house?"

"They are lost in their own grief, caught in a web of their own memories. Some may seek vengeance or recognition for thei pain, while others are simply searching for their peace." Adeline's gaze turned slightly somber. "You must tread carefully, each spirit holds their own power over their own story, and the spirit world of this place is not without its dangers."

"What kind of dangers?" Ella asked, her unease growing.

"Anger can manifest into mere darkness. Spirits filled with past rage may lash out at you, unwilling to let go of their suffering here. You must approach them with much compassion, determination, but be very cautious of their mere intentions."

With another deep breath, trying to keep herself calm, Ella steeled herself, "I will be careful, Adeline. How can I help them all find their peace?"

"Listen," Adeline instructed. "Create a safe space for them to share their stories with you. They need to feel seen and heard, just as you would. Their fragile memories can lead to their mere healing, both for them and for you."

Ella felt the weight of Adeline's words, "I will do it, I will try my best to do it." She promised, "But I need to know more about your family, whatever you can remember will help me. What were their names?

Adeline's expression softened, "My parents were Eliza and Thomas. I had a brother, Thomas Junior, and a sister, Clara. We were a very close family, and the fire... it shattered us." A slight flicker of mere pain crossed over Adeline's fragile face, and Ella felt her heart ache for the spirit.

"Can you somehow show me?" Ella asked gently, desperate to understand.

Adeline only nodded, and the room began to shimmer around them. Ella felt herself being drawn into a vision, a whirl of chaos and sensations swirling all around her. Suddenly, she was standing in a grand living room, its walls adorned with rich, colorful tapestries and painted family portraits. A soothing fire crackled warmly in the hearth, and faint laughter echoed through the air. Ella looked around in awe, recognizing the mere room as a part of her own home, yet slightly different now, but very much alive with light and energy. Children played on the massive rug while Adeline's parents watched fondly from their cozy seats, their faces beaming with much joy.

"Look closer," Adeline urged, her faint voice resonating in Ella's mind.

Ella seemed to move closer to the hearth, the mere fireplace, where a large, family portrait hung, capturing a moment frozen in time. In the painting, she saw Adeline as a child, her innocent smile radiating happiness. Eliza, a woman with kind eyes, stood beside Adeline, while her father held a small Thomas Junior in his arms, with Clara peeking out from behind her mother's skirt, her mere face a mix of mischief and delight. This painting was very similar to the old photograph, yet it seemed they were all slightly older in the old photo. But then, the vision shifted abruptly. Shadows, dark and creepy, began to creep in from the corners, engulfing the warmth of the scene, the vision. Ella watched in horror as heavy smoke filled the living room, the mere laughter turning into screams. The entire family was trapped in the chaos, confusion, great fear written on their faces.

"Adeline!" Ella shouted, feeling the weight of the horror. "What happened? What caused the fire?"

"I do not know. They were all taken by surprise," Adeline said, her faint voice trembling, "The massive fire spread faster than they could escape, including me. I was the last to see them, the last to save them, but I could not, the fire consumed me as well. That was my last memory of them."

The scene, suddenly, shifted again, now showing Adeline frantically running through the manor, the thick smoke curling around her. Ella felt a deep sense of loss, tragedy, as she watched Adeline struggle against the cruel flames, her desperate attempts to save herself and her family echoing through the smoky air. And then, just as quickly as it had begun, the vision faded, leaving Ella breathless and shaken. She found herself back in the guest room, the pillar candle still flickering gently before her. Adeline was still in front of her, tears glimmering in her ghostly eyes.

"I couldn't save them." Adeline whispered faintly, her voice breaking, "I couldn't bring them back."

Ella's heart ached for the young spirit, "You did everything you could, but now, you need to tell your story. You need to help your family, and you find peace."

Adeline nodded, a flicker of hope igniting in her fragile gaze, "You are right. I have held onto my pain for too long. It is time to share our stories and release our sorrows."

As Ella felt the energy shift in the room, she realized that this quest was not just about helping Adeline; it was about embracing the mere connections between the past and the present, life and death. The spirit world within this old house was not just a place of fear but a tapestry of untold stories just waiting to be woven together, where healing could be found in the mere act of remembrance.

"Let's do it together, Adeline," Ella said, determination filling her heart, as if the spirit was still alive. "We will gather all the other spirits within this house, and we will listen to their stories, one by one, we will help them find their peace."

Adeline smiled, the warmth returning to her mere presence, "Thank you, Ella. You are more than I could have ever hoped for in a friend. Together, we will bridge the thin gap between our realms, our worlds."

With that, the two of them began to forge an estranged connection deeper than either could have imagined, a bond that would lead them to uncover the myriad tales woven into the fabric of Willow Creek Manor, bringing light to the darkest corners of the spirit world within the house.

Chapter 5

Haunting of My Dreams

That night, Ella fell into a deep sleep, the events of the day swirling in her mind like autumn leaves caught in a breeze. She had spent hours poring over old records, uncovering stories of the families that once filled Willow Creek with much laughter and vibrant life. Now, with the fragile spirit, Adeline, guiding her, she felt a sense of renewed purpose stirring deep within her, but a tinge of anxiety lingered at the edges of her consciousness. As she drifted into slumber, her dreams took her to a place where the spiritual veil between worlds was very thin. She found herself standing in a shadowy version of her master bedroom, the candles flickering, casting eerie shadows on the faded walls. The mere atmosphere was thick with palpable tension, and Ella's heart raced.

Suddenly, she heard faint whispers, echoes at first but growing ever so louder, flowing through the space of the room like a haunting melody, "Ella..." they called, voices overlapping in a cacophony of much longing and utter despair.

"Who's there?" she asked, feeling a cold chill crawl up her spine, "Adeline?"

From the darkness emerged a figure, not Adeline, but a man with sorrowful eyes and a weary expression. He wore a long coat, tattered at the edges, and a hat pulled low over his brow, "I am Thomas," he said, his voice heavy with grief. "Adeline's father."

Ella's breath caught in her throat. "You're... you are here... in this house? How can I help you?"

"Help us all remember," he simply pleaded, his faint gaze piercing through her. "We are all lost in our mere, faint memories, trapped between what was and what could have been. My family... we deserve to remember, to be remembered."

"I can help you, sir. I am trying." Ella replied, her resolve strengthening. "Tell me your side of the story. I truly want to listen."

As she spoke, the room around her shifted again, morphing into a scene from the past. Ella stood in the same living room she had seen before, but now it was alive with lovely colors and vibrant laughter. Thomas was there, a masculine man full of life, sitting on the wooden floor with his small children. Young Clara was playfully tugging at Adeline's hair, while Thomas junior sat nearby, engrossed in a series of giggles as he kicked and played with his fragile, small hands. Ella felt a warmth envelope her, a stark contrast to the somber reality of Thomas's fate, his mere ghostly figure, but just as quickly, the scene began to darken, the joyous laughter fading into terrified screams. Heavy, thick smoke billowed in from the corners, and the happy family became frantic, scrambling for mere safety.

"No!" Ella cried out, her heart breaking as she watched the horror unfold. Thomas's face twisted with utter despair as he tried to gather his fragile, helpless children, but intense flames consumed the entire room around them.

"Adeline!" he shouted, panic seeping into his voice. "We must get her out!"

Just as the chaos reached its peak, Ella was yanked from the vision of her dream, landing back in her shadowy master bedroom. The faint whispers grew louder, mingling with the mere sound of crackling flames, echoing within her mind. She was trapped in a cycle of nightmares, the spirits' anguish invading her dreams. "Ella!" a new voice broke through the tumult. It was young Clara, her youthful voice filled with urgency. "You must find us, help us! We need to be remembered!"

"Clara?" Ella's voice trembled as she felt the weight of despair pressing against her chest. "How do I find you; how do I help you?"

"Gather our memories," young Clara implored. "Share our laughter, our love. Let the world know that we lived, that we mattered."

As the dream shifted again, Ella found herself standing in the middle of a beautiful garden, vibrant with many colorful flowers that bloomed in every hue imaginable. The sun beamed brightly, casting a warm, soothing glow that felt like a mere hug. Thomas, Adeline, and Clara appeared before her, their faces radiant with such life. "Tell them of our beautiful garden," Adeline said, stepping forward. "We would spend hours together here, laughing, playing. This is where we felt truly alive."

Ella nodded, understanding, "I will remember. I will tell your stories, and I will make sure others know the joy, the love you all shared."

Just as quickly as the scene had brightened, it began to fade. The lovely garden transformed into a darkened room, shadows creeping back in as the whispers grew louder again. Ella felt a slight panic rising within her, "No! Please, stay with me! Don't go!"

"Just remember us!" they called out in unison, their faint voices intertwining with the haunting echoes of their past. "Remember our love! We are not just a mere tragedy; we are a family!"

Suddenly, Ella jolted fully awake, her heart racing, her forehead full of warm sweat. The master bedroom was dim, the fragile pillar candle still flickering gently on her bedside table. She sat up in her bed, her mind swirling with fragments of the unsettling dream, the mere laughter, that lovely garden, the mere horror of the massive fire. Gasping for breath, she slowly calmed her nerves, realizing that this was only just the beginning. These spirits needed her to gather their memories, their stories, to weave together their past memories of much joy and utter pain, and to help them all find their peace. She couldn't let their voices fade into the dark shadows of this manor, being trapped for far too long. She had to somehow honor their lives.

Determined, Ella pulled out her journal and began to write, capturing every detail of her dream, the garden, the laughter, the family bonds that had been forged in love but shattered by great tragedy. Each word felt like a lifeline thrown to the fragile spirits, a way to actually honor them all and keep their stories alive.

As the first light of dawn broke through the window, Ella felt a sense of accomplishment. She would visit the garden that Adeline's spirit had showed her in her dream, a place where the spirits had actually found much joy. There, she would gather her thoughts and prepare for the quest that still laid ahead, a mere journey of simple remembrance and healing. Today would mark the actual beginning of her true commitment to the spirits, the sweet family of Willow Creek Manor. She would listen, remember, and share their stories, bringing light into their dark shadowed eternity that lingered within the walls of her manor. The haunting of her dreams would guide her on, lighting the path toward understanding, and she was ready to embrace whatever came next.

Chapter 6

The Demon in the Attic

As the sun climbed higher in the sky, Ella felt a renewed sense of determination. She gathered all her notes and set off toward the attic of her old house, a place she had yet looked at. The next step in her quest to help Adeline and her family. The dusty, creepy attic felt like a forbidden realm, shrouded in mere mystery and darkness, but she knew that to truly understand more to the history of Willow Creek, she needed to confront whatever may lay ahead, even if it meant something might be hidden in the attic.

Climbing the narrow, wooden staircase, the mere air grew colder, the wood creaking beneath her feet as she ascended. A heavy door loomed at the top, its surface scarred and severely weathered. Taking a deep breath, Ella pushed it open, the antique hinges groaning in much protest. Inside, the attic was a treasure trove of many forgotten old, relics, draped with dust and cobwebs. Old trunks and boxes filled the vacant space, remnants of lives lived long ago. Ella felt a thrill of frightful anticipation mingled with trepidation, but as she stepped fully inside the attic, a chill enveloped over her, snaking its way up her spine.

Suddenly, a low growl reverberated through the space, sending a terrifying shiver through her bones. Ella froze, her heart pounding heavily. She strained her ears, and the growl transformed into a raspy voice, very deep and resonant. "You should not be here..."

"Who's there?" Ella called out, trying to steady her breath, hoping it was just another mere spirit in need of help, but this voice felt different, evil. "Show yourself!"

From the shadows, a dark figure emerged, a tall creature with dark, twisted features, its eyes glowing like fire, like hot embers. It seemed writhe in the dim lighting of the attic, a grotesque silhouette against the cobwebbed walls. The air grew heavy with malice, and Ella felt an instinctual fear rising within her.

"I am the keeper of this place, this house," it seemed to his, its mere voice a chilling whisper that echoed loudly through the attic, "And you are an intruder. You are not wanted here."

"I'm not an intruder; I own this manor. I am not here to cause trouble, but to help the spirits to find their peace." Ella replied, summoning her courage, "I am searching for the truth about this very house, the untold stories that need to be told."

The creature let out a low, rumbling laugh. "Stories? You think you can unearth the forgotten past? The lives that were cruelly lost? They all belong to me now, except for one, the small boy was set free. I could not hold his innocent soul. They are my mere shadows, my prisoners to this house. I will not let them go."

Ella's heart became frightful as she felt the weight of these horrid words, "You are a demon," she stated, fear and realization intertwining. "You feed off of their pain, off of their fear, but I am not afraid of you."

The demon tilted its head, intrigued. "You are bold for a mere mortal girl, but boldness does not shield you from my darkness. This house has suffered; it cradles all its ghosts trapped here, and I merely thrive on their eternal torment."

"I am here to help them, to set them free," Ella declared, her voice gaining strength. "They deserve to be remembered, not consumed by your evil darkness."

The demon snarled, shadows flickering around it like flames in a fire, "You think you can banish me? They are bound to me, and I will not relinquish my hold on them."

Ella felt a surge of brave determination rise within her, though she was truly terrified. "You don't understand. Their stories hold all the power. They can't be trapped by fear, by you, any longer; they deserve to be free, to find their peace."

With that, she reached into her pocket and pulled out her journal, the pages filled with all the memories she had begun to gather. "I will honor all the spirits trapped in this house; I will free them." She said fiercely. "I will tell all their stories, and in doing so, I will shine a light into your mere darkness."

As Ella began to read aloud the scribbled words in her journal that she had recently written, the mere atmosphere shifted. The shadows around the gruesome demon writhed and twisted violently, as if recoiling from the light of her voice. The growls turned into hisses, and the creature's form began to flicker. "No!" it roared, its mere voice filled with rage, "You cannot take them all from me!"

But Ella pressed on, focused, recounting all the laughter of the loving, ghostly family from the garden, the warmth of their unconditional love, the joy that had once filled the old manor's walls. Each word that she spoke was a beacon, pushing back against the dark shadows, illuminating the attic with a warm, soothing glow. The cruel demon faltered, its mere form wavering as Ella continued. "Adeline, Thomas, the father, Eliza, the mother, Clara, and Thomas Junior... they all lived, they all loved. You cannot extinguish their light!"

With each name that Ella spoke, the demon shrank back, its form distorting, writhing in much protest, much anger. Ella felt the mere energy shift in the room of the attic, the weight of despair lifting as the loving memories surged forth, filling the attic with warmth and hope.

"You think you can save them?" the awful demon spat, desperation creeping into its voice. "They are mine!"

"No," Ella asserted, her voice firm, strong, and unwavering. "They are not yours, not anymore. They belong to the world, to their own stories, their own destinies, and I will make sure they are remembered."

With one final push, Ella closed her eyes, focusing on the mere love that now filled the attic, their memories that she had gathered in her journal. She visualized the loving spirits that now stood with her, united against the darkness, the twisted demon, along with the spirit's laughter and joy creating a strong barrier of light.

"Together, we will set them free, find their peace," Ella declared, her voice ringing clear. "And you will fade into nothing, you cruel fiend."

As her words echoed through the attic, the demon let out a deafening roar, its form twisting more and unraveling, the dark shadows retreating like a tide. Ella felt the heat of its anger wash over her, but she stood firm, her heart filled with the spirits' strength. With one flash of bright light, the cruel demon shattered, dissipating into the ether like smoke caught in a breeze. The attic fell silent, the oppressive weight merely lifting as warmth flooded the entire room. Ella stood alone now, dark and quiet, panting, but victorious. In the stillness that followed, she felt a gentle breeze, a gentle presence at her side. Turning, she saw Adeline, her spirit glowing with much gratitude. "You did it, Ella. You freed us all from its grasp."

Ella smiled, tears of relief and joy brimming her eyes. "We did it together, Adeline. Your family's stories will always be remembered now."

Adeline's expression was serene, a peaceful smile crossing her lips. "Thank you so much for standing up for all of us. You have given us hope in our eternity, and now we can finally find rest in this afterlife."

As the light of dawn began to filter through the attic window, Ella felt a sense of closure wash over her. She had faced the evil darkness and emerged stronger, not only for herself but for the sweet spirits that had long lingered in the mere shadows of this old house.

"Let's tell the entire world about you and your family," Ella said softly. "Your laughter, your love... it deserves to be celebrated, remembered."

Adeline nodded in agreement, her fragile, ghostly form fading, leaving behind a sense of peace and light that now filled the attic. Ella took a deep breath of relief, knowing the mere journey was far from over, but invigorated by the simple knowledge that she could actually make a difference. She slowly descended the staircase, the echoes of faint laughter and love resonating within her heart. The small battle with the demon had opened a new chapter, one where she could honor the spirits of Willow Creek Manor and share their stories with the world. As she stepped into the sunlight, she knew she was ready for whatever may come next within this old house... a journey not just of remembrance, but of great healing for both the living and the lost.

Chapter 7

The Broken Doll

As the days passed after her intense confrontation with the cruel demon in the attic, Ella felt a renewed sense of purpose. She was determined to gather and share the stories of the spirits tied to Willow Creek, and she knew that her next step simply involved uncovering more of their past, their history.

One afternoon, while rummaging through the old wooden trunks in the attic, Ella stumbled upon a small, ornate box tucked away in a deserted corner. Intrigued, she brushed off the dust and opened it. Inside lay a delicate porcelain doll, its once vibrant dress now faded and severely tattered, a small crack running down one cheek of the fragile doll. The glass doll had a haunting beauty to it, its glassy blue eyes staring up at her as if it held many secrets waiting to be unveiled. "Who do you belong to?" Ella whispered, a slight shiver running down her spine as she lifted the doll from the damaged box. She could almost feel the weight of sadness that surrounded it, the sad connection, vibe it gave off, a mere palpable reminder of lost innocence of the past.

As she examined the fragile doll more closely, the atmosphere shifted, and a soft, childlike voice echoed in her mind, "Please... please don't leave me here."

Startled, Ella looked around the attic, searching for the source of the faint voice, "Who's there?" she called out, gripping the broken doll tightly.

"It's me, Clara." the voice said, and suddenly the air shimmered, revealing a small figure standing by the window of the attic. Clara's spirit was a luminous silhouette, her fragile, small face a mere mix of hope and sorrow.

"Clara!" Ella exclaimed, her heart swelling with much recognition. "You're here! I think I found your doll..."

The childlike spirit nodded, her faint expression shifting as she glanced at the fragile, tattered doll in Ella's hands. "I loved her so much, but when the fire came, I had lost her... and everything else."

"I'm so sorry, Clara," Ella said softly, her heart aching for the young girl, "But we can remember you, your tale, and you do not have to be lost anymore."

"Can you help me fix her?" Clara's faint voice trembled with such longing as she gazed at her doll. "I want to see her whole again, like she was when I first got her from my father."

Ella glanced down at the doll, its severely cracked porcelain seeming to reflect Clara's own fragmented spirit. "Of course, I will try... I will do everything I can, but we really need to hear your story, share your tale first. You deserve to be remembered."

Clara's ghostly eyes brighted, "I want to tell you my story, about my family. We played here, in this house. I remember the garden outside, the laughs we shared together... but the fire stole it all from us."

Ella felt the mere pull of Clara's memories, and with a gentle nod, she invited the small spirit to share her story. "Please, tell me what you remember, Clara."

The attic shifted once more, transforming into a vibrant vision, a scene of the garden that Ella had glimpsed in her earlier visions. Sunlight filtered through the leaves, casting dappled shadows on the ground where Clara once played, her laughter ringing like sweet music in the air. "I loved to play here with my brother, Thomas Junior," Clara began, her sweet voice filling the space. "We'd pretend we were adventurers, exploring the many wonders of our garden. Adeline would, often, join us, and we'd pick wildflowers and roses for our mother."

As she spoke, Ella could see the joyful scene unfold before her. Adeline, a radiant young girl, young woman, twirled in a flowery dress, while Thomas Junior chased after a butterfly, his boyish laughter bubbling over. The essence of happiness filled the air, a stark contrast of the darkness that had so long haunted this family.

"But then, one day..." Clara's voice faltered, the brightness dimming, "The fire came. I thought we could escape it, but I couldn't find my doll. I went back into the house to get her, but the smoke was too thick, I could not see... the smoke was everywhere."

Ella's heart broke, ached as she watched Clara's spirit fade, the mere joy slipping away as she spoke of her fear, "I lost everything that day." Clara continued, tears shimmering in her fragile, ghostly eyes. "My mother, my father, my entire family... my home... and my doll."

As the memory settled in the attic, Ella could feel Clara's pain, her sorrow, washing over her like a cold wave. "You are so brave, Clara, for sharing this with me," Ella said gently, "Your love for your family and your doll is still alive. It doesn't have to be forgotten now."

"But I can't be whole without her," Clara whispered, glancing at the tattered doll in Ella's hands. "I've searched for her for so long... will you help me fix her?"

"Yes, absolutely, Clara." Ella promised, determination filling her heart. "I will make sure she is whole again, and in doing so, we will honor your story."

With that, the attic shifted the vision once more, the surroundings fading to reveal a dimly lit workshop filled with various supplies, paints, brushes, and threads of many colors. Clara's spirit flickered with such excitement, and Ella could feel the energy of creation swirling around them. "Let's do this together, Clara," Ella said, feeling a sense of warmth and a sweet, inner connection as she set to work. Carefully, she began to slowly mend the tattered doll, applying fresh paint to the small cracks, stitching the fragile dress, and restoring its delicate features in this vision. Each small brushstroke felt like a whisper of love, a mere tribute to Clara and her little family.

As the doll took shape, the mere atmosphere brightened, the shadows receding like a morning mist. Clara watched with wide eyes; her spirit glowing as Ella breathed new life into the cherished object.

"I can feel it!" Clara exclaimed, her faint, childish voice filled with much joy. "She's coming back to me, my lost doll!"

With the final touch, Ella placed the fragile, porcelain doll upright in Clara's tiny hands. "She is whole again, Clara, just like you will be now," she said, her heart swelling with hope.

Clara gazed at the fragile doll, her ghostly eyes shifting with glimmering tears of happiness. "Thank you, Miss Ella! Thank you for helping me find my doll! Thank you for remembering us!"

Ella felt a rush of warmth enveloping the attic, and the spirits of Adeline, Thomas, and Thomas Junior appeared around Clara, their mere expressions filled with pure love and much gratitude. Together, they formed a circle of light, a small testament to the bonds that had endured even in death.

"Your family will always be remembered, Clara," Ella promised, her voice steady. "Your laughter, your adventures in the flower garden, they will live on through your stories."

As the spirits began to shimmer, Clara's form glowed brighter, the joy radiating from her. "I can feel them, all of us together again. Thank you for giving us this moment, for allowing us to be whole again. We just need Mother now."

With that, the loving spirits began to fade, their laughter echoing softly in the attic. Clara held her fragile doll close, her mere spirit a beacon of light, reflecting the love that had once filled Willow Creek. Ella stood alone now in the dimness of the attic, a sense of peace washing over her. The weight of Clara's small tale, the beauty of their connection, had transformed the entire room. She realized that each spirit she had encountered had a story that was worth telling, a small piece of the past, of history, that needed to be honored. Now, she had to hear the mother's story, wherever she may roam in this old manor. Determined, Ella gathered the old tattered doll from the floor of the attic and placed it back into the old ornate box, a tangible reminder of Clara's spirit and the love that transcended time. Clara was at peace now as well as the others, Ella would share their entire story with the world, weaving it into the tapestry of Willow Creek's history. As she descended the attic stairs, Ella felt the warmth of Clara's faint laughter still resonating in her heart. Each small tale, each memory she uncovered, would be a mere light against any darkness, a way to honor not only the spirits of the past but the love that would forever connect them all.

Chapter 8

The Woman Who Makes The Soup

Ella awoke the next morning with Clara's sweet laughter still echoing in her mind. The mere experience of restoring the fragile doll had filled her with gratitude and hope, much energy of happiness, and she was eager to continue her journey in this old manor, of uncovering the rest of the untold stories of Willow Creek. Today, she felt a pull toward the kitchen, where the scent of something warm and inviting seemed to linger in the air, almost like a vegetable soup being cooked, almost as if it were beckoning her.

As she entered the vacant kitchen, she was enveloped by the familiar aromas of herbs and spices, although the room appeared empty. The old wooden table was cluttered with a few faded recipe cards, some stained and worn, hinting at the many meals that were prepared there. Ella reached out to touch the surface of the table, tracing her fingers over the faded patterns that were etched into the wood, the marks left by hands that had cooked and shared meals here for generations. Suddenly, a soft, feminine voice broke the stillness, "Ah, it's you, my dear."

Startled, Ella turned to see a woman standing in the corner of the kitchen. She was dressed in a simple but elegant dress, her hair tied back in a tight bun, and she had a warm, nurturing smile that radiated comfort. "I am Eliza," she introduced herself, her ghostly eyes sparkling with kindness.

"Are you... are you the spirit of the mother to Adeline and Clara?" Ella asked, a mix of awe and curiosity bubbling within her.

"Indeed, I am," Eliza replied, her smile deepening. "I once filled this very kitchen with much love and warmth, making soups and stews to nourish my family, my babies. Food has a way of connecting us all, don't you think?"

"Yes, it does, I suppose," Ella agreed, feeling the weight of Eliza's ghostly presence. "I've been gathering your family's stories. I met Clara and I restored her fragile, porcelain doll."

A flicker of sadness crossed Eliza's face, "My sweet girls, Clara and Adeline. Clara always loved that doll. She brought much joy to our humble home, even as the shadows grew closer. My sweet baby boy, Thomas Junior, I feel has already moved on... I miss him so much."

Ella nodded, understanding the mere gravity of what Eliza had lost, "I want to help you. Your family's story deserves to be told, you deserve to find your peace."

Eliza's ghostly expression brightened, "Thank you, my dear, but first, let me share with you the secrets of my soup recipe. It's more than just a meal; it's a reflection of our love, our memory, and our connection."

With that, Eliza moved to the unused stove, her spirit gliding effortlessly as she began to gather her ingredients that seemed to magically appear from thin air. Ella watched this vision, mesmerized, as

Eliza chopped vegetables with deft hands and stirred the bubbling iron pot. The fragrant steam rose, filling the kitchen with a sense of warmth that felt like a comforting embrace. The mere aroma of the soup filled Ella's nostrils.

"Every ingredient has a story," Eliza said, glancing back at Ella with a knowing smile. "Onions for the tears we have shed, carrots for the sweetness of our memories, and herbs for the love we shared."

Ella leaned closer, captivated by the whole process. "What exactly do you mean?"

"When we cook, we infuse our mere emotions into the food. Each bite carries a piece of us, our joys, our sorrows. It's a way to honor those who came before us." Eliza paused, her faint gaze drifting to the window where sunlight streamed in. "And in sharing our meals, we keep their spirits alive."

As the soup simmered, Eliza continued, her faint voice a melodic whisper, "After the massive fire, the kitchen was one of the last places I wanted to return, but I found my solace in the act of cooking, in nourishing the souls of those still with me, even in spirit. I cook in hopes of luring my family back to me one day."

Ella felt a wave of slight understanding wash over her, "You turned your pain into something beautiful."

"Yes, dear, and now, it is your turn to share my story." Eliza stirred the pot, her mere movements graceful and deliberate. "I want you to taste it, my soup, to feel what we felt as a family."

With that, Ella ladled the rich soup into a bowl and handed it to Ella. The moment Ella took a sip, she was transported into a memory. The flavors danced on her tongue, rich and savory, evoking images of a bustling family gathering in the same kitchen, children laughing, the warmth of the fire crackling, and the smell of fresh bread baking. "Remember this feeling, my dear," Eliza urged, her ghostly eyes sparkling with much wisdom, "When you tell our story, let it be filled with the love that we once shared over our meals together, the small laughs that echoed off these very walls around this table."

Ella closed her eyes, allowing the memory to wash over her. She saw Thomas, the father, and Eliza working side by side, the children bustling around them, setting the table, and giggling as they helped. It was a moment frozen in time, filled with warmth and belonging. When she opened her eyes, she found Eliza watching her, a gentle smile gracing her lips. "You see? Our love in this family can transcend time, even the darkest of times."

"Yes, I see that," Ella breathed, feeling the weight of Eliza's words settle deep in her heart. "I will make sure your family's story is told, and I will include all the love that went into every meal, every moment shared."

"Thank you, my dear," Eliza said softly. "In doing so, you will nourish the hearts of those who hear our tale, just as the soup nourished my loving family."

As the sun dipped lower in the sky, casting a golden hue across the kitchen, Ella felt a sense of fulfillment swell within her. She understood now that each spirit within this manor that she encountered was a mere thread in the tapestry of Willow Creek, woven together by love, much loss, and the past memories that still lingered.

"Before you go," Eliza said, her faint voice imbued with kindness, "take this with you." She handed Ella a small jar filled with dried herbs. "These are from my garden. Use them in your cooking and remember to infuse your meals with genuine love."

Ella accepted the jar of herbs, feeling the weight of Eliza's gift, "I will always cherish it," she promised.

As she turned to leave the kitchen, it began to shimmer brightly, and Eliza's spirit glowed with an ethereal light. "Remember, my dear, that love is the most powerful ingredient. It can heal, connect, and transcend time."

With those words echoing in her mind, her heart, Ella stepped out of the kitchen, carrying with her the warmth of Eliza's sweet, kind, spirit and the promise of the stories yet to unfold. The mere journey to honor all the spirits of Willow Creek was still far from over, and she felt a renewed determination to share all their tales, to weave together the threads of such love and their memory that would create a lasting legacy. Ella couldn't wait to write this experience in the kitchen down in her journal.

Chapter 9

The Violent Spirit

Ella had always known that not all spirits were gentle or nurturing. After her encounters with Clara and Eliza, she felt a sense of caution creeping in. Each story had been filled with much warmth and kindness, but now a new, darker energy brushed against the edges of her awareness, a darker feeling, a darker presence that seemed to lurk in the shadows of Willow Creek Manor.

That evening, as she sat in the living room pouring over all her notes, writing the spirit's stories in her journal, a chill swept over her, through the mere air, causing the hairs on the back of her neck to stand up. The flickering candlelight seemed to dance more violently, casting eerie, erratic shadows to twist along the walls. "Who's there?" Ella cried out, trying to steady her shaking voice, "Show yourself!"

But instead of a gentle spirit, the mere atmosphere thickened with great tension, an oppressive weight that made her chest feel tight. The temperature dropped suddenly, sharply, and she could see her breath misting in the air of the living room. Then, a loud crash echoed from the attic, followed by a guttural growl that reverberated through the entire house.

Ella's heart raced as she stood quickly, instinctively knowing she had to confront whatever was causing all the disturbance. Climbing the stairs, cautiously, the mere air grew heavier, charged with an unsettling energy. The door to the attic creaked open, revealing a scene of complete chaos... boxes were overturned, and the remnants of her earlier explorations were scattered across the old, wooden floor. In the faint corner of the room, a dark shadow writhed and twisted miserably, the outline of a dark figure emerging from the darkness. It was unlike any spirit Ella had ever encountered thus far, its form was jagged and distorted, its eyes were glowing like fiery coals, radiating much rage and despair.

"Leave this place!" it roared, the sound echoing like thunder in the confined attic.

"Why are you here?" Ella, though shaken, managed to ask, her voice trembling but resolute. "What do you want?"

"I am the spirit of mere wrath, girl," it hissed, the dark shadows around it swirling like smoke from a fire. "I was wronged, severely, in my mortal life, betrayed by those I once trusted. I have been condemned to this wretched house, this miserable place, and I will not let anyone find any peace here!"

Ella took a cautious step back, the weight of the spirit's anger, its rage, palpable. "I am here to help all the spirits trapped in this old house. I want to understand your sorrow, your pain, your past."

"Help?" the spirit laughed, a harsh sound that sent chills down her spine. "You cannot help me! I am bound by the rage of my cruel death, a fury that completely consumes me!"

Ella felt a strange surge of compassion for this violent spirit, "But holding on to that rage of the past only keeps you trapped. You can find your peace; you just need to let the past go."

"Let go?" the angry spirit spat; its voice laced with much bitterness. "You think I haven't tried? The flames of betrayal still burn in my dead heart! All I really want is revenge!"

Suddenly, a violent gust of wind swirled through the attic, knocking over more boxes and sending random papers flying in all directions. Ella struggled to keep her footing, the spirit's anger manifesting in brutal chaos all around her.

"Calm down!" Ella shouted, frustrated, her voice rising above all the commotion and noise. "You don't have to keep hurting yourself, or others! You can just share your painful story with me instead!"

"Share my story?" the angry spirit sneered, but Ella could see a small flicker of uncertainty in its fiery gaze. "No one would truly listen. No one would truly care about the wronged, or the saddened."

"Well, I care!" Ella shouted, insisting, as her heart raced in frustration, "You deserve to be heard. Just tell me what happened to you, and I promise I will listen; I will remember your tale."

For a brief moment, the angry spirit hesitated, its fury momentarily subdued by a slight glimmer of vulnerability. "I was once a proud, masculine man, a leader in this very town. I trusted my closest friend, but he betrayed me, taking what was rightfully mine. I died alone, consumed by my anger."

Ella sensed a small shift in the hectic atmosphere, "Your anger has kept you trapped in this vicious cycle of such violence within this manor for so long. You can be free, but you have to confront that pain."

"Free?" The spirit's voice broke, cracked, the flames in its eyes dimming. "What does freedom even mean when I was never given justice?"

"Justice can come in many different forms," Ella replied gently, caring, "Sharing your story, letting go of the need for revenge... that kind of justice, it honors you. It honors your memory and allows you to find your peace."

The spirit's form flickered, and Ella saw faint flashes of a man... once proud, handsome, now shattered by mere betrayal. "I don't know if I can let go completely," the spirit murmured, the growl in its voice softening. "The pain is really all I have left."

Ella took a small step closer, sensing the spirit's turmoil. "You can transform that bitter pain into something else, something honorable. You can honor your life as it was and the legacy that you wanted to leave behind. Your tragic story can be a lesson for others in this world of life."

The dark shadow wavered, caught in the struggle between anger and the mere desire for such release of the past. "But how, exactly?" it whispered, the fight in its voice dimming, calming.

"Start by telling me your name," Ella encouraged. "Let's reclaim your true identity. Who you were before the cruel betrayal."

"Samuel," the spirit finally admitted, its voice barely above a whisper, "I was Samuel, a man who wanted to do good for his entire community."

"Then let's honor that, Samuel," Ella said, her voice steady, calm. "Tell me more about your story, your dreams, your hopes for this town. Let's bring some light to your story."

As she spoke, the air began to shift again, the oppressive energy slowly lifting. Samuel's form flickered, and the mere anger that had consumed him started to dissipate, revealing a glimpse of humanity beneath the rage. "I wanted to build a place for everyone in this town, a refuge," he began, his voice trembling as he remembered, "But all I built was a prison for myself, trapped in my own anger. I wanted to be remembered for my success, my kindness, not my wrath."

"Yes!" Ella encouraged, her heart swelling with hope for the spirit. "Let's share that story. Your kindness does matter. Your legacy can live on through your mere actions and words now."

As Samuel recounted his dreams, his hopes, for the community, the mere chaos around them settled down, the dark shadows softening. With each word, the tension in the attic slowly lifted, replaced by a sense of release and much relief. "Thank you, Samuel said, his voice now a gentle, humbled murmur. "For allowing me to remember who I was. I didn't think I could ever again share my story, my pain, my sorrow without it consuming me."

"You can change your pain and sorrow into wisdom, Samuel," Ella said softly. "You've done that here, now. You can find your peace."

The dark shadows no longer lingered, merely turning into light, as they glowed, illuminating his human form as he began to dissolve, his anger lifting, gone, like fog in the morning light. "I will remember," he whispered, his voice fading. "Thank you for reminding me of the great man that I once was."

As the last remnants of Samuel's spirit vanished into a peaceful haze, Ella felt a profound sense of accomplishment wash over her. She had faced the darkness of this violent spirit and helped this tormented soul find the light, its peace. The attic was now quiet, the chaos replaced by a serene stillness. Ella descended the stairs, her heart brimming with the knowledge that even the most violent of spirits could find solace. She would continue to honor the many stories of Willow Creek, weaving together the tales of love, and such loss, as well as the redemption, reminding the world that even in the darkest of times, tragedies, there was always a path that leads to healing. Ella had to retrieve her journal and record this encounter.

Chapter 10

The Sad Eyes

After the encounter with the angry, violent spirit, Samuel, Ella felt a sense of triumph and purpose, yet a lingering heaviness still hung in the air of the old manor. It was as if the old house itself held its breath, waiting for the next experience, the next story to emerge from the shadows. Ella sensed another faint spirit nearby... one that was not filled with bad energy or anger, but rather much sorrow, sadness.

Later into the evening, while Ella sat in the parlor writing Samuel's tale into her journal, she was drawn to a faint, shadowy figure in the corner of the room. It stood silently, its fragile presence barely noticeable, except for the profound sadness that seemed to emanate from it. As she approached, slowly, the figure materialized into a young woman with soft features and hauntingly sad eyes.

"Hello," Ella said gently, taking a cautious step closer. "I can see you; I won't hurt you. What's your name?"

The fragile woman's lips trembled as she spoke, "I am Margaret," she faintly replied, her voice a fragile whisper. "I've been waiting for someone to notice me."

"I'm here, Margaret, and I notice you." Ella assured her, her heart aching for the fragile spirit, at the mere sorrow that was reflected in Margaret's sad eyes. "What keeps you here?"

"I do not know how to explain it," Margaret said, her voice quavering, "I have been lost in my grief for so long. I watched the world move on without me, and it feels like I have become a mere shadow of my past."

Ella felt the mere weight of Margaret's sadness pressing down on her. "What happened to you, Margaret?"

The fragile spirit looked down, her fingers fidgeting with the old hem of her ethereal dress. "I lost my child, my baby... a daughter. She was taken from me too soon. I never had the chance to say goodbye."

Ella's heart broke into pieces at the admission, "I am so sorry, Margaret. That must be so incredibly painful for you."

"It it, it truly is." Margaret said, as tears glistened in her sad eyes. "I thought I could protect her, but I failed. Now, I'm left with nothing but this heartache. I wander these very halls, trapped in my pain, my sorrow, unable to find my child, or my peace."

"I want to help you, Margaret, I can try to help you," Ella offered, her voice, calm, yet steady despite the sad heaviness of the moment. "I may not can reunite you to your daughter, but your baby does deserve to be remembered. You deserve to share your story, your love for her."

Margaret's sad eyes met Ella's, filled with a slight ray of some hope, "You would do that for me? For us, my daughter?"

"Of course, I would." Ella affirmed. "Tell me about your child, what was her name?"

"Lily," Margaret whispered, her voice barely audible. "She was full of life, laughter, and much joy. She loved to look around in the garden, especially the roses, while I held her in my arms. Every day, I would pick a rose for her to place in her crib, just a small gesture of love that filled my heart with such happiness.

As Margaret spoke, the air shifted, and Ella could almost see the vibrant image of a young child, a young girl, dancing with her baby in her arms through the beautiful flower garden, sunlight playing off her golden curls. "Tell me more about Lily," Ella encouraged, leaning in closer.

"She was adventurous," Margaret continued, her voice gaining strength. "Always crawling, exploring, always finding the beauty in the smallest things. I remember one day, she came crawling over to me while we were in the living room of this house, her tiny hands full of flower petals that I had placed on her blanket in the floor. My Lily smiled revealing the one fragile tooth she had, as she threw the petals into the air, crawling back to her blanket." A bittersweet smile crossed Margaret's face as she reminisced, "In those precious moments, I felt like the luckiest mother alive."

"Those sweet memories really are precious," Ella said softly. "Your love for your daughter, Lily, is very much still alive in you, and it deserves to be shared."

"But how can I actually move on, find my peace?" Margaret asked, sadly, her sadness returning. "I feel like I am betraying my Lily, her memory, by letting go of my grief."

Ella took a deep breath, searching for the right words, "Grief is merely a testament to your love for your daughter, but it doesn't have to consume you. Sharing Lily's story, her memory, and celebrating her spirit... that is how you can honor her."

Margaret's expression softened, the weight of her sorrow mingling with the warmth of her memories. "You truly believe that?"

"I do," Ella replied, her heart swelling with much compassion. "You can carry Lily's memory with you, not just in your grief but in the joy, she had brought you. Let her laughter fill your heart once more."

As the saddened spirit considered Ella's words, the room brightened, the faint shadows lifting as the warmth of such love began to fill the space. "I remember the last time I held her," Margaret said, her voice trembling. "She hugged me tight as I whispered, 'I love you, forever and always.'"

Tears streamed down Margaret's ghostly cheeks, but this time, they were mingled with a slight sense of release. "I want to remember my Lily in that way, as she smiles back at me."

"Then, that is exactly what you should do," Ella said, her voice confident, soothing. "Let's honor you and Lily, always. Tell me more... her favorite toy, the stories she loved to hear the most, and the way she made you feel complete."

As Margaret shared many more tales about her daughter, Lily, Ella felt the energy shift again all around the room. The air became lighter, filled with more warmth and love. They spoke of Lily's favorite songs to hear, her childish laughter that echoed through the halls of this old house, and the way she would smile as her mom would dance around with her in her arms. Margaret's mere spirit becoming brighter and unyielding. With each sweet memory, Margaret began to transform. The sadness in her fragile eyes was replaced by a glimmer of joy, and the faint shadows that clung to her began to dissipate. "Thank you," the sad spirit whispered, her voice slightly stronger now. "You've helped me remember the light, the happiness, not just the darkness and the sorrow."

As the final words of their conversation lingered within the room, Margaret began to glow, her sweet, fragile form radiating a gentle warmth. "I can feel her spirit with me now, my Lily. She remains in my heart. Thank you for giving me this gift."

Ella smiled, feeling a wave of happiness wash over her. "You deserve to find your peace, Margaret. Lily will always be a part of you, and her love will never fade."

With a final, grateful smile, Margaret's spirit began to fade, the faint shadows dissolving into a soft light. "I will always remember," she whispered, her fragile voice echoing like a gentle breeze. "Thank you so much for reminding me that love is eternal."

As Margaret's presence vanished, Ella stood alone in the parlor, the air filled with such warmth and light. The old house felt much different now, the mere heaviness of it, now lifted, replaced by a sense of peace and healing. In that moment, Ella fully understood that every spirit had a story to tell... some, a story of love, some of loss, and some of hope. She was determined to continue to honor all their memories, weaving their tales into the very fabric of Willow Creek Manor. The journey was now over, yet each encounter brought her closer to more understanding of the true essence of all the spirits she had come to know. Ella continued to write all their stories into her journal.

Chapter 11

Looking Back... Unexplained

As Ella settled into her favorite chair by the window of her room, the sun dipped low on the horizon, casting a warm glow across Willow Creek. The old house felt alive with so many memories, each room whispering the many stories of all the spirits she had encountered thus far... Clara's laughter, Eliza's warmth, motherly love, Adeline's sweetness and her entire family, along with Samuel's transformation, and Margaret's love for her daughter, Lily, it filled the air within the old house with such love, like symphony of sweet voices, reminding her of the profound journey she had undertaken.

With each spirit she helped, she had uncovered not just their histories but also the deeper truths about their love, their grief, and their healing. Yet, as she reflected on her experiences, she couldn't shake the mere feeling that something still remained... an unexplained connection within the old house that lingered in the faint corners of her mind. The memories of her experiences with the spirits flooded back to her: the way the attic had shifted, the vibrant garden where

Clara had played with her family, her siblings, and the warmth of Eliza's kitchen. Each spirit had left an imprint on her heart, a mere reminder of the fragility and beauty of life.

Ella pulled her journal out, the pages already filled with all the stories, the tales, and sketches of all her encounters. She smiled as she traced her fingers over the words, but something nagged at her, an unanswered question that had yet to find its resolution. 'What was the source of all these connections, these encounters? Why had she been the one chosen to uncover all their stories and help them to find their peace?'

Just then, a flicker of movement caught her eye from the corner of the bedroom. Ella turned, and there, against the backdrop of the fading light, was a bright figure that she had not seen before. The spirit was soothing, dressed in flowing robes that seemed to ripple like mist. Its eyes were deep and knowing, they seemed to hold much wisdom that made Ella's heart race.

"Who are you?" she asked, curiosity mingling with apprehension.

"I am the Keeper of Stories, the Angel of the Lost," the spirit replied, its kind voice resonating like a soothing chime. "I am here to guide those who seek to understand the truths hidden within the mere threads of life and death."

Ella felt a rush of recognition, her pulse quickening. "You've been watching over all the spirits that I have encountered in this old manor?"

"Indeed," the Keeper said, stepping closer, its presence both comforting and inspiring. "Each spirit you have met and helped was simply drawn to your empathy, your inner desire to connect and heal, to remember their love. You have given them a voice, a mere chance to be remembered, and in doing so, you have woven their untold stories into the very fabric of this place, this manor."

"But why me?" Ella asked, her heart pounding. "What is it about me that made this all possible?"

The Keeper smiled softly, as if understanding the mere weight of her sincere question. "Every soul carries within it the potential for connection, the ability to bridge the thin gap between the living and the departed. You have chosen to embrace that potential, to seek the understanding rather than fear it."

Ella's mind raced, "So, this isn't just about Willow Creek? This is much bigger?'

"Yes, it very vast," the Keeper replied, its voice echoing with a timeless wisdom. "You are part of a larger tapestry woven together by the mere stories of all who have come before. By honoring their memories, you also honor your own journey, your own pain and grief, and your own healing."

Ella felt a deep sense of resonance. The old house, all the spirits, their stories... it was all intertwined, a reflection of her own life and struggles. "I never thought of it in that way," she admitted, her voice barely above a whisper.

The Keeper's expression shifted, growing slightly serious. "Though, there are many souls in need of a voice, Ella, your journey is now over. You helped them who were lost, you helped them find their peace, to find their way to the light."

"I tried my best to guide them to their eternal peace," Ella said, as uncertainty crept into her thoughts. "I really tried to help them move on."

"By remaining open-minded," the Keeper replied, its eyes glowing with an ancient light. "you continued to listen, to connect, and to share their stories. You merely trusted your inner intuition, and the mere memory of your own healing shall come now."

As the Keeper spoke, Ella felt a surge of renewed hope welling within her. She had already uncovered so much, but there was still a vastness of stories waiting to be told, to be shared. "I want to remember," she said firmly, determination igniting her own spirit.

"Then you will," the Keeper replied, its form beginning to fade into the gathering twilight. "Remember, every spirit is a mere guide, a simple reminder of the love and connection that can transcend time. Keep your heart open, and you will never walk alone. You shall remember."

With those final words, the Keeper vanished, leaving Ella in the gentle embrace of the dusk. The room felt different now, suffused with an energy of possibility and hope. She looked around, the famliar spaces infused with new meaning. Each room of this old manor, each shadow, was a reminder that life was not just a series of unforgotten moments, but a tapestry woven with much love, loss, and the mere stories that lingered. As she gazed out the bedroom window, the stars began to twinkle brighter against the darkening sky. Ella smiled softly, a sense of peace washing over her. She couldn't continue this journey any longer, she had honored all the spirits of Willow Creek Manor, sharing their stories, and embracing the inknown. The path ahead was both exhilarating and mysterious, but she knew she was now ready to face it. She remembered...

Her own story... that had held her to this old house, Ella and her husband had purchased this manor, this lovely, old home years ago. It was not her husband who was gone, but her. She was the one who was lost. It was her who had died in this old house from a mere fever, a sickness. Ella's memories flooded in, as she remembered seeing her husband leave the place, as he looked back at this very bedroom window where she stood and said, "I will always love you, my sweet Ella."

In the end, life, like all the spirits she had come to know, was full of unanswered questions, yet it was precisely those little mysteries that made it beautiful. Ella understood that while she may never fully grasp the depth of their experiences in this old house, she could celebrate their lives by listening, learning, and sharing, exactly what she had done for them. With her heart full of love and peacefulness now, she prepared for whatever eternity awaited her, ready to uncover the unexplained and embrace the magic that lay just beyond the veil...

Ella stepped into the light, the abyss... Willow Creek Manor was forever empty.

"Looking Back... Unexplained" (Collection of Ghostly Tales and Haunts)

"Looking Back... Unexplained"
(Collection of Ghostly Tales
and Haunts)

By: Jo Ann Atcheson Gray